Living
With Others

Living With Others

(Preteen Bible Exploration #2)

Leslie H. Stobbe

MOTT MEDIA

LIVING WITH OTHERS

Illustrated by Ruth A. Wick
Edited by Leonard George Goss
Typeset by Suzanne DePodesta, Karen White and
    Joyce Bohn

Printed in the United States of America

ISBN 0-88062-114-1

Contents

Welcome Aboard, Explorer

What's tougher than swimming across Lake Michigan, pitching a no-hitter, knitting an Irish fisherman's sweater, scoring twenty points in a basketball game?

No, it isn't going to the moon! The hardest things you'll ever do are to get along with

    a younger brother or sister
    father and mother
    a teacher
    the kid two houses down
    the bully on your street
    the show-off in your grade

the handicapped child
a kid with another racial background.

Can studying the Bible help you with getting along with others, with developing relationships (as we adults call them)? I won't give you a quick answer to that, for as an explorer it is your job to find out the answer.

All of the Bible explorations let you see what kinds of difficulties Bible people got into, and what Jesus said about getting along with others. And the stories about kids on your street help you see how the ideas you'll discover in your exploration might work in real life.

All you will need for this exploration is your favorite Bible, a notebook, and a pen or pencil. Don't try to do all the exploration at once. And if you need help I'm sure your Dad or Mom (or even an older brother or sister) will be happy to help you.

A Word to Parents

Here's the second book in a series designed to help your preteen begin an exciting exploration of the Bible. You, too, will enjoy the study, for it focuses on biblical patterns of relating to other people. In tackling the exploration with your preteen you will undoubtedly also develop new and exciting dimensions in your relationship with him or her.

If you have already done the Bible exploration in *Preteen Bible Exploration #1*, you will know that a modern translation of the Bible is recommended. You may, in fact, want to have a paraphrase like the Living Bible handy as well so your preteen can read it in language more familiar to him or her.

Do not let the exploration become a chore, and do not let it drag on after your preteen has obviously lost interest for that day. On some days concern for a friend, an assignment in school, or a bad day in his relationship with you can prevent a fruitful exploration. Don't worry, your preteen will feel better emotionally on another day and may then truly enjoy an exploration of a biblical character.

Always remember that the Bible is the Word of God. Because it is God communicating to us it has the power to change our attitudes and behavior. That is why preteens should begin Bible exploration, rather than waiting until they get into high school or college.

Happy exploring!

1

You Promised

The day had been hot and muggy. The evening didn't bring any cool air either. Just walking up the front steps had made Carl perspire. Now that supper was over he just wanted to sit and watch TV. So he grabbed a tall glass, threw in a couple of ice cubes, added some coke, and headed for the family room.

Carl had taken only three steps in the direction of the family room when Don, three years younger, burst into the kitchen.

"Carl, will you play catch with me now?" he asked.

Carl looked at the cool glass of coke in his hand, thought of the comedy and detective story on TV and curtly replied, "No, go find Jim."

Yet Don wasn't about to give up. He adored his older brother and loved playing catch with him.

"Aw c'mon. You promised!"

Carl didn't hesitate for a moment.

"Forget it. It's too hot."

"But you promised," pleaded Don persistently.

At that moment Carl swept into the family room, leaving his brother frustrated and angry in the kitchen.

"But he promised," Don muttered as he dejectedly headed for the back door.

When is a promise really a promise? Is it important to keep a promise? Let's check out what happens when you make a promise to someone. One of the greatest men of faith who ever lived can show us what may happen if we really want to keep our promise, our commitment, to God.

Who Promised What?

Ever tell someone, "You promised," and have him say, "I did not"? You're sure you remember exactly what he promised, but he says again that he cannot remember making a promise. Maybe he honestly cannot remember making the promise. Or maybe you forgot who really made the promise.

Abraham never forgot who had made him a promise. That's why he kept his promises to God.

You don't remember who Abraham was? Turn to Genesis 13: 1-6.

Day 1.   What suggests that Abraham was not a poor man?

Day 2.   How do we know that Abraham was a religious person?

Day 3.   Who was with Abraham? Now turn to Genesis 17:1-8 to see what God promised him.

Day 4. How old was Abraham when God made His promise?

Day 5. How does God identify Himself?

Day 6. What tells us that there would be many grandchildren in Abraham's family? Verse 6.

Day 7. What land does God promise to give Abraham? Verse 8.

Day 8. What is God's special promise to Abraham? Verse 7.

A Special Promise

When Carl made his promise to play catch with Don it may have been a cool day. Or maybe he sort of half made the promise so Don would stop bothering him. Maybe Carl was walking with a friend and wanted to talk about some special things that Don shouldn't hear. He made a promise to get rid of his brother. It was not a special promise.

God had a very special promise for Abraham. We read about it in Genesis 17:15-19.

Day 9. What is God's promise to Abraham in verse 16?

Day 10. What is Abraham's reaction?

Day 11. How does God make sure Abraham really understands the promise? Verse 19.

Day 12. How many children is Isaac going to have? Compare verse 19 with Genesis 13:16. Well, they aren't really going to be his children, but also his children's children, and then their children.

A Promise Kept

It's one thing to make a promise. But it is

sometimes very hard to keep it. When God told Abraham he and Sarah would have a son, Abraham was 100 years old and Sarah 90 years old. Both Abraham and Sarah laughed when God made the promise, thinking it was impossible for them as old people to have a son. But what happened?

Day 13.   Turn to Genesis 21:1-8. What happened to Sarah?

Day 14.   What name did Abraham give his son? Verse 3.

Day 15.   How do we know Sarah remembered laughing when God made the promise? Verse 6.

Day 16.   How do we know Abraham was proud of his son? Verse 8.

A Test

When Don came into the kitchen to try to get Carl to play catch with him, it was a test. What kind of test? Don was checking whether Carl would keep a promise. Did Carl pass the test?

Day 17.   Sometimes God tests us to see if we really believe He will keep His promise . . . and to see if we will keep our promise to serve Him. What is God doing to Abraham in Genesis 22:1?

Day 18.   Keep your Bible open to chapter 22. What special thing does God want Abraham to do? Verse 2.

Day 19.   How many sons did Abraham have by this time? Verse 2.

Day 20.   How do we know that Abraham was to be alone with Isaac when he sacrificed him? Verse 2.

Day 21. When did Abraham leave to carry out God's command? Verse 3.

Day 22. What tells us that Abraham really meant to make a sacrifice? Verse 3.

Day 23. How many days did they travel to the place God had chosen? Verse 4.

Day 24. How did Abraham make sure he would be with Isaac? Verse 5.

Day 25. What were he and Isaac going to do? See verse 5. Since a sacrifice was an act of worship, Abraham was really telling the truth.

Day 26. Who had to carry the wood for the fire of sacrifice?

Day 27.   Did Isaac get suspicious? Verse 7. How did Abraham answer?

Day 28.   How do we know Abraham was really willing to do what God had asked him to do? Verses 9 and 10.

Day 29.   How does God stop the sacrifice? Verses 11 and 12.

Day 30.   Now that God knew that Abraham was truly loyal to him, that he really was willing to trust God, what did God do? Verse 13.

Do you think Abraham ever thought, *Does God really have to make it so hard to keep my promise to serve Him?* Probably, but for Abraham a promise was a promise. Why?

Read verse 8 again. God had kept His promise to Abraham by giving him a son. If he had kept that promise, surely He would provide some way to save Isaac's life.

Think back. Would it have been hard for Carl to keep his promise to Don? Oh sure, he would have had a lot of sweat to wipe off, he would have been super warm. Yet just because it is hard doesn't mean we should break our promise. After all, we want others to keep their promises to us, don't we?

2

Fooling Father

The basketball arched through the air, dropping through the basket with barely a ripple on the string. Burt grabbed it and dribbled to the outer edge of the key, turned and shot. His ball arched, too, but it fell a couple of feet short of the basket.

Some day I'm going to be as good as one of the players on the Harlem Globetrotters, he thought, retrieving the ball again. He could still hear his father.

"Burt, I know you'd like to see the Harlem Globetrotters when they come to our city in December. I'll make a bargain with you. You get a B average on your report card and I will take you. Sound okay to you?"

Dad had ruffled his hair and given him a pat on the shoulder.

"I know you can do it."

Burt wasn't so sure. He knew his marks had not

been good recently. He couldn't seem to get excited about studies with the new teacher. But going to see the Harlem Globetrotters sure would be nice. . . .

An Assignment

Burt faced a challenge. He'd have to work hard to please his father, but he knew that his Dad kept his word. Let's read about another son who received a challenge from his father. Turn to Genesis chapter 27.

Day 1.   What is Isaac's physical handicap? Verse 1.

Day 2.   Whom did he call to his side? Verse 1.

Day 3.   What was the special job Isaac gave to Esau? Verses 2 and 3.

Day 4.   How was Esau supposed to prepare the game he hunted? Verse 4. Why should he bring it to Isaac that way?

Day 5.   Who is Rebekah? Can you guess from chapter 26, verse 35?

Day 6.   What had Rebekah overheard? Back to chapter 27, verses 5-7.

Day 7.   What did Rebekah want Jacob to do? Verse 8 and 9.

Day 8.   What would Rebekah do with the kids (baby goats)? Verse 9.

Day 9.   Why would she do this? Verse 10.

A Bit of Trickery

Just as Burt shot at the basket for the 99th time he had an idea. He could hardly wait to carry it out. He dropped the ball in the box and hurried to his

friend Steve's house. Steve wouldn't be caught dead on the basketball court after school. He was too busy studying.

Burt knocked on the door. Steve's mother answered.

"May I see Steve?" Burt asked.

"Sure, come in. You look like you've had quite a workout. Have you been shooting baskets?" she asked as she opened the door and let Burt in.

"The usual," Steve said casually as he stepped in.

Day 10. What was Jacob's problem about the whole thing? Verse 11.

Day 11. How do we know he thought it was wrong? Verse 12. What did he think might be the result of trying to fool his Dad?

Day 12. What excuse did his mother give him? Verse 13.

Day 13. Did Jacob obey his conscience and do what he thought was right? Verse 14.

Day 14. What part did his mother play? Verses 15-17.

Day 15. How do we know Jacob was a pretty good actor? Verses 18-20.

Day 16. What tells us that Jacob had been taught about God? Verse 20.

Day 17. How did Isaac try to make sure that this was really his son Esau? Verse 21-24.

Day 18. How do we know that Isaac really loved his son Esau? Verses 25-27.

Day 19. What is the blessing Isaac now gives his son Jacob, who he thought was Esau? Verses 27-29.

Trickery Unmasked

"Steve, can you help me with my project at school?" Burt asked when he arrived at Steve's room. "I'm just no good at projects, and you are so good at it."

Steve was flattered. He knew Burt was one of the best basketball players in school. He also knew that Burt had a tough time with their new teacher.

"Sure, I'll help you."

They worked on the project at Steve's house every day after Burt had finished basketball practice. Burt knew that the new teacher would really like the work Steve was doing on the project and that would help him with his grades. His father would never know!

Day 20. How soon did Esau arrive after Jacob had left Isaac? Verses 30-32.

Day 21. What shows us that Isaac knew how serious the deceit of Jacob had been? Verse 33.

Day 22. What is Esau's reaction? Verse 34.

Day 23. What does Isaac have to tell his favorite son? Verse 35.

Day 24. How does Esau react when he hears what has happened? Verse 36.

Day 25. What was left for Esau? Verse 37. How did this affect Esau's feelings toward Jacob? Verse 41.

Finally the day for the report cards arrived. Burt could hardly wait. He quickly looked at his when he got it. Even though there was a C on it, he also had an A in Social Studies because the teacher had really liked the project. Wait until his Dad saw that!

Day 26. How did Jacob get the news about how his brother felt? Verse 42.

Day 27. What would Jacob have to do to escape his brother's anger? Verses 43-44.

Day 28. What scheme did Rebekah dream up to get Jacob sent away to her brother? Verse 46.

Day 29. How do we know that Isaac forgave his son? Chapter 28:1-3.

Day 30. What special blessing does he call upon Jacob? Verse 4.

"Burt, my father is taking me to the Harlem Globetrotter game. He told me that he and your Dad bought tickets next to each other," Steve announced a couple of days later. Burt was glad he could go with Steve.

During an intermission at the game Steve's father turned to Burt's father, "You know, that was a beautiful project Steve did with Burt. Steve put a lot of work into it."

Burt almost swallowed his bubble gum. He looked at Steve and realized that he was not aware of anything wrong.

"Great," said Burt's Dad. "Burt got an A on his report card because of it."

That's all he said, even though Burt knew his Dad must have caught on to what he had done.

That evening after they had walked into the house Dad turned to Burt, "I thought you said *you* had done that project?"

Burt knew it was time to 'fess up, and he did.

"You've got your reward, and I won't take the joy of being at the game away from you. Remember, however, that the Bible says, 'Be sure your sins will find you out,' " his father said.

Burt threw his arms around his father.

"I love you, Dad. I'm so glad we could go to the game together. And I promise not to try to fool you again."

3

The Troubleshooter

The hot sun beat unmercifully down on the plain. Shimmering heat waves danced across the land. Around a greener section sheep lay after a day of grazing. Men went about the early evening tasks of preparing for a meal and the approaching night.

Suddenly one of them noticed some movement on the horizon. What at first appeared to be a dot grew larger and larger.

"Look," said Judah. "It's a man. Who would be out along at this time of day?"

Several men got up to look at the strange scene. In this area you just didn't see a man alone. There were too many wild animals. Only caravans, groups of men on camels carrying trade goods, came through this region.

"Judah, look again," exclaimed Simeon. "I think that's our famous younger brother. Wonder what fancy story he's got for us this time. He sure thinks he's the greatest, doesn't he?"

"Yes, and I think we can take care of him this time. He's so far away from father that we'll just let him disappear and no one will be the wiser," another brother chimed in.

"I say we kill him and throw him into one of the pits," added another.

Guess who the hated brother was? Time to go exploring in the Bible and see what happened. Look up Genesis 37:2 and see who it is. Let's find out if all the brothers were equally hateful to Joseph. Did you ever wonder if maybe there was at least one brother who stuck up for Joseph?

When Hate Boils Over

Gerry was the new boy at school. He wasn't only from the next town or state. He had come from another country! And here he was trying to be part of the gang on the schoolyard at lunch.

Out of the corner of his eye Gerry saw a whispered conference. The boys came running toward him. Suddenly they stooped and began picking up snow, forming snowballs. Gerry saw he was in trouble and turned to head for the school, but he was slow to escape. A shower of snowballs smacked on his jacket, pants, neck and head.

The boys laughed derisively as they threw again and again at the stumbling, retreating boy.

What did Gerry need at this time? Now turn to Genesis 37:12.

Day 1. Who was sent to check on his brothers for his father? Verse 13.

Day 2. Why was Joseph sent? Verse 14.

Day 3. What had happened when Joseph went to the place where his brothers had been pasturing their flock?

Day 4. Where did Joseph find his brothers? Verse17.

Day 5. What did Joseph's brothers decide to do when they saw him coming? Verse 18.

Day 6. What nickname did they give Joseph? Verse 19.

Day 7. Had Joseph earned that nickname? Why? See Verses 5 to 7.

Day 8. How were they going to cover-up the murder of their brother? Verse 20.

A Better Idea

Suppose one of the boys in Gerry's schoolyard had run up to the fellows starting to throw snowballs and said, "Don't. You might hurt him." Do you think they would have listened to him? What could he have said that might have stopped them? Let's see what happened to Joseph.

Day 9. Give the name of the brother who speaks up. What place does he have in the family? See Genesis 37:21 and 22.

Day 10. As the oldest in the family, Reuben had quite a bit of authority. When he said something, brothers were supposed to listen. What does he say they should not do? Verse 21.

Day 11. What does he suggest they do instead? Verse 22.

Day 12. What are Reuben's secret plans? Verse 22.

Day 13.   Read verse 22 again. What do you like about Reuben's attitude toward Joseph? What can we learn about our attitude toward our brother and our father?

Day 14.   What is the first thing that happens to Joseph when he reaches his brothers? Verse 23. Why did they do that? Look back at verse 3.

Day 15.   What did they do to him next? Verse 24.

Day 16.   What was the pit, or hole in the ground, like when they put Joseph into it? Verse 24.

Trouble on the Way

Remember Gerry? You're on the playground and see the snowballs start to fly. You know they won't stop if you put up your hand like a policeman and say, "Stop, you're hurting Gerry!" What did Reuben do? He suggested a new and different activity. What could you suggest to the boys to distract them and draw their attention away from Gerry? Then the bell rings and everybody heads for the building before your idea can be carried out. What might happen at recess?

Day 17.   What did Joseph's brothers do once they had dropped him out of sight? Verse 25.

Day 18.   Do you think they sent one of the brothers with a plate of food for Joseph? Why not?

Day 19.   Who shows up now? Verse 25.

Day 20.   Why were they traveling this route? Verse 25.

Day 21.   What were they going to sell in Egypt? Verse 25. Do you think they had any slaves to sell as well?

Day 22. Who is the businessman among the brothers? Verse 26. What is he concerned about?

Day 23. What does Judah suggest they do instead of killing Joseph? Verse 26.

Day 24. What reason does he give for selling Joseph instead of killing him? Verse 27.

Day 25. For how much profit did Joseph's brothers sell him to the traders? Verse 28.

Day 26. Where did the traders take Joseph? Verse 28.

Day 27. How do we know Reuben was not there when Joseph was lifted out of the pit and sold to the traders? Verse 29 and 30.

The Brothers Meet Again

Joseph becomes a very important man in Egypt. He is put in charge of the food supply during seven years of drought and famine. His brothers travel to Egypt to get grain. It's a great story and you should read it in Genesis 42 to 45, but for now let's find out about some interesting things that happened to the brothers who helped sell Joseph.

Day 28. Joseph had accused his brothers of

being spies and put them in prison for three days. Then he suggested one of them stay in prison while they go home and bring the youngest brother, Benjamin. How did Joseph find out what really happened when his brothers put him in the pit? Verses 21 to 24 of chapter 42.

Day 29.   Normally the oldest brother would have been put in prison because he is the most important in the family. Yet Joseph put the second oldest in prison. Why was Simeon put in prison instead of Reuben, who was the oldest? Read verses 22-24 again.

Day 30.   Joseph spared Reuben the pain of imprisonment because he now knew Reuben had stood up for him. Yet another brother was involved in the sale of Joseph. Remember who suggested it? Turn to Genesis 37:26 if you've forgotten.

Day 31.   The family had used up all the grain Joseph had given them. It was time to go again . . . and get Simeon out of jail. But to release Simeon, Joseph had said they had to bring Benjamin. Their father, Jacob, didn't like the idea of sending Benjamin to Egypt. Read Genesis 43:8-9. Judah seems to have learned an important lesson. We are responsible for others, especially those in our family. Once he had sold Joseph to traders because he hated him so much. Now he was willing to be responsible for the safety of Benjamin. That he actually does feel responsible is seen in Genesis 44:14-34.

You're on your way out to the playground at recess. You see Gerry just a little ahead of you. You know the fellows who threw the snowballs at him may try something else. What do you do? What do you think Jesus would want you to do?

4

As the
Sword Flies

Jim was very proud of his snow fort. He and Bill had worked on it many hours, cutting blocks of snow from the settled section and piling them up for a large wall. They could hide behind it, pretending they were fighting off Indian attacks.

But one day Tim rushed outside on his way to school and glanced in the direction of the fort. It was smashed! Someone had knocked over the whole wall.

He was sure he knew who had done it. There was only one group in the neighborhood who would do a thing like that. When he saw Bill come out of his house, he rushed up to him.

"Do you know what those kids on Locust Street did? They've smashed our fort. I'm going to get even with them!" Tim said angrily.

"How do you know they did it?" asked Bill.

"I know they did it. They're the only guys who would be so mean. Every time we build something nice they try to wreck it," Tim answered hotly.

Together they hurried off to school, plotting revenge.

By the time school was out Tim and Bill had plans to get even. When summer came the kids on Locust Street always set up a tent in one the boys' back yard. Some day while the gang was off to the ice cream store, Tim and Bill would pull the tent pegs out and collapse the tent!

This month we want to read about a great chance to get even.

Being Chased

Turn to 1 Samuel 24:22.

Day 1.   The story really starts with chapter 23, verse 24. Who was being chased by King Saul?

Day 2.   Why couldn't King Saul encircle David and capture him? Verse 26 to 28.

Day 3.   Why was King Saul able to chase David again? Verse 1 of chapter 24.

Day 4.   Where was David hiding out?

Day 5.   How many soldiers did King Saul take with him to try to capture David? Verse 2.

Day 6.   How many men were with David in the wilderness? See chapter 22, verse 2.

Day 7.   Where was David hiding on this particular day? Verse 3.

A Cloak and Dagger Mission

Tim and Bill knew that if they went to the Locust

Street tent and destroyed it, the gang would be so angry they would beat them up. Also, the gang would know who had done it since it was so soon after Tim and Bill's fort had been destroyed. So how could they get even without being hurt again?

First they had to let the gang forget that they had destroyed Tim and Bill's fort. They had to let it seem like they weren't planning revenge. Only then would they have the slightest chance of collapsing the tent and getting away with it.

Apparently King Saul went to sleep near the front of the cave unaware that his enemy was hiding deep in the cave. His guards may have been outside of the cave. Here was David's chance! Did he take it?

Day 8.   Whose idea was it to take care of King Saul once and for all? Verse 4.

Day 9.   What did David do when he had super-quietly crept to where King Saul lay, with his kingly robe lying beside him? Verse 4.

Day 10.   David had been so close to King Saul that he could easily have killed him. Yet how did he feel about even cutting off a piece of the king's robe? Verse 5.

Day 11.   Why didn't David kill his enemy when he had the chance? Verse 6.

Day 12.   How do we know David's followers were not pleased with David's unwillingness to hurt King Saul, even though the king had set out to kill them all? Verse 7.

Day 13.   Did King Saul know anything about how close he came to being killed? Verse 7.

Day 14.   Was David a brave man? Verse 8.

Day 15.   How did David honor King Saul even though the king had set out to kill him? Verse 9.
Day 16.   Who helped make King Saul even more jealous and afraid of David? Verse 9.
Day 17.   How do we know David could have killed King Saul? Verse 10.
Day 18.   Why didn't David kill the king? Verse 10.
Day 19.   What proof does David offer that he could have killed King Saul? Verse 11.

Who's the Judge?

Tim looked over the row of boys waiting to be picked for a game of baseball. As an outstanding catcher, he had been asked to be captain of one team. He had already chosen Bill for his team, since Bill was a good pitcher. He had also chosen Ed for first base, Ted for second base, Ike for shortstop, and Mike for third base. They were all his friends and he could depend on them to play hard for him.

Now he was out of good friends. In the line-up was the leader of the Locust Street guys, and two members of the gang. All three were good ballplayers. They could be a strong outfield. But Tim still remembered what they had done to his fort! It would serve them right if no one chose them! Why should he give them a chance to show how good they were?

Yet, it was a tough decision.

David had made the decision not to kill his enemy. Would it really make a difference?

Day 20.   Who should judge how King Saul should be punished for his attempts to kill David? Verse 12.

Day 21. What proverb does David quote to the king? Verse 13. What does the proverb mean?

Day 22. How weak does David feel in light of the large armed force King Saul brought with him? Verse 14.

Day 23. Who does David call on to be his "lawyer" and "judge?" Verse 15.

Day 24. How does King Saul react to David's little speech? Verse 16.

Day 25. What does King Saul say about David? Verse 17.

Day 26. How did David "turn the other cheek?" Verse 18.

Day 27. How do we know King Saul recognizes how fortunate he is to be alive after David had the chance to kill him? Verse 19.

Day 28. King Saul suddenly realizes that he is fighting in vain against the man God has chosen to be king. How do we know that? Verse 20.

Day 29. What does King Saul ask David not to do when he becomes king? Verse 21. (It was common for a new king to kill all the sons of the king before him.)

Day 30.   How did King Saul and David sign the new peace agreement? Verse 22.

Tim suddenly knew what he had to do. He was a Christian and he could not hold a grudge. He had to "turn the other cheek" and choose the members of the Locust Street gang for his team.

And guess what? When he chose them he suddenly lost his urge to collapse their tent. God had taken the anger out of his heart.

5

Toughing It

Tom and Philip moved away from the group of boys. The teacher had named them captains of the ball teams. They could each select their players, taking turns.

"Heads or tails," the teacher asked Tom.

"Tails," he said as the teacher flipped the coin and let it fall on the ground.

"Philip gets first choice," the teacher said, confirming that the coin had come down heads up.

Though Max was the tallest in the group he stood off to one side. He knew that he would be chosen last. Not only was he a poor player, he was also cross-eyed. He watched enviously as Tom and Philip chose their best friends for their teams. Sure enough, Max and two others were extras when the teams were full and told to sit and watch. He decided to cheer for Philip's team, since he liked Philip better.

Have you ever been chosen last? Then take courage, for one of the Bible's great heroes was once chosen last. Turn to 1 Samuel 16 and 17 for today's Bible exploration.

Time to Choose

God had chosen Saul to be king over the people in Israel. He loved God and served him for several years. Then he got to feeling very important. One day he did not obey God and tried to cover up.

Day 1.   Why was Samuel supposed to go and choose a new king for Israel? 1 Samuel 16:1.

Day 2.   What was the cover-up for Samuel's mission? Verses 2-5.

Day 3.   How many sons of Jesse were brought before Samuel so he could choose one as king from among them? Verses 6-10.

Day 4.   Why did God not choose any of them as the next king? Verse 7.

Day 5.   What was son number eight doing while the rest were parading before Samuel, the prophet of God? Verse 11.

Day 6.   Why did the father, Jesse, not consider David important enough to be part of the dinner? Verse 11.

Day 7.   Why is it so surprising that Father Jesse had not introduced David to Samuel? Verse 12.

Day 8.   What did Samuel do that probably made David's brothers envious? Verse 13.

Day 9.   How do we know that David was important to God? Verse 13.

Important Mission

Max decided that he would show the rest of the boys a thing or two. Because he was tall he started practicing high jumping. Sure enough, he was chosen by the teacher to compete in the annual area-wide track meet. What a thrill to ride the bus to the school where the meet was held, since he lived so close to school he never got a ride on the school bus. But an even bigger thrill was being third in the high jumping competition. He proudly wore the third place ribbon as he rode home on the bus.

Day 10. What happened when Saul was disobedient to God? Verse 14.

Day 11. What did King Saul's men suggest might soothe the king's spirit? Verses 15 and 16.

Day 12. What was the king's reaction to this idea? Verse 17.

Day 13. How does the servant of King Saul describe David? Verse 18.

Day 14. What did David bring along as a special gift for the king? Verses 19-20.

Day 15. How do we know that King Saul was impressed by this shepherd boy? Verse 21.

Day 16. In what way did David help to soothe the bad moods of King Saul? Verse 23. What brought on these bad moods?

Mission Impossible

"Cross-eyes!"
"Fatty!"
"Stumpy!"
How Max hated those names. Every day the kids

seemed to come up with a new nickname for him. Many times he wished he could hide and never show up again. One day his mother said to him, "Max, we are going to take you to a special kind of doctor. He thinks he can help straighten out your eyes."

Max was happy, even though he knew the treatment could be painful. Yet he also wondered if even this would help him. That seemed like mission impossible.

Day 17.   Who came to fight against King Saul and the people of Israel? 1 Samuel 17:1-2.

Day 18.   What kind of line-up did the armies have? Verse 3.

Day 19.   Who was the champion fighter for the Philistines? Verses 4-7.

Day 20.   What did he say to the soldiers in King Saul's army? Verses 8-10.

Day 21.   How many of David's brothers were in the army facing Goliath? Verses 12-14.

Day 22.   What was David doing during this time? Verse 15.

Day 23.   What did David's father ask him to do? Verses 17-19.

Day 24.   What did David do when he found the armies? Verses 20-22.

Day 25.   What scary sight did David see when he was looking for his brothers? Verses 23-24.

Day 26.   Why did David not run away like the other soldiers? Verses 26-27.

Day 27.   How do we know David's brothers looked down on him as a useless nobody, good only to herd sheep? Verse 28.

Day 28.   How did Saul react when he heard the questions David was asking? Verses 29-31.

Day 29.   What were David's reasons for not being afraid to fight Goliath? Verses 32-37.

Day 30.   How did David approach the fight with Goliath? Verses 38-40. What was Goliath's reaction to the sight of the shepherd boy? Verses 42-44.

Day 31.   What proves that David's God was mightier than the strength of the giant? Verses 45-51. What do you think his brothers thought of David now?

Just like David, Max prayed that God would help the doctor straighten out his eyes. And God did. God used Max to bring the good news of Jesus to many people and helped him win many battles. He learned that it is not how you look or how important others think you are, but how much you trust God to help you.

6

King's Orders

Suppose you were given $100 and told, "I want you to do something special for someone. Pick anyone you like, but use this money to give him a good time." Whom would you choose?

- Your best friend at school?
- Your best friend at Stockade?
- The boy down the street who doesn't seem to have any friends?
- Your little brother who always wants to tag along when you want to play with your best friend?
- The boy around the corner who gets about in a wheelchair?

You can't really do much with $100, but it would be fun anyway, wouldn't it? But now suppose you are king of Israel and Judah. Your army has been fighting your worst enemy, the Philistines, and has been winning battles. So you have good hopes of being king for a while.

On top of that God has made a special promise to you. It sounds too good to be true, but you know God keeps His promises. Let's see what happened – and then see what we can do to help people.

An Unfortunate Accident

Remember King Saul? He was the first king of Israel and was so tall he could have been center on Israel's national basketball team. But he forgot that God had made him king. He started doing things his own way, so God said He would make David king instead. In a big battle with the Philistines both King Saul and his son, Jonathan, were killed. Actually, King Saul killed himself because he didn't want to be captured by the Philistines. Now read what happened to one of the sons of Jonathan in 2 Samuel 4:4.

Day 1.   What is the name of Jonathan's son?

Day 2.   What kind of a physical problem did Mephibosheth have?

Day 3.   How did Mephibosheth get hurt? Those were the days when they didn't have special jobs for the handicapped or crippled. So the chances of Mephibosheth making a living on his own were small.

Day 4.   Now read about King David in 2 Samuel 7:8-11.

Day 5.   Name three things God promised to King David.

Day 6.   How long was David's kingdom to be? Verse 12.

Time to Help Someone

When is it the most fun to help someone? When you've just lost a ballgame? Or when you've won a no-hitter? David was now firmly in control in Israel, even though at one time he had been a fugitive from King Saul. Now was the time to be generous.

Day 7. Whose family was David concerned about? 2 Samuel 9:1.

Day 8. Why did King David want to be generous to someone in King Saul's family? Verse 1. If you cannot remember who Jonathan was, read 1 Samuel 20.

Day 9. Whom did they find from the household of Saul? 2 Samuel 9:1.

Day 10. Whose servant had Ziba been? Verse 2.

Day 11. What does King David want to do? Verse 3.

Day 12. What was Ziba's reply? Verse 3. Remember how he was crippled? See 2 Samuel 4:4 if you have forgotten.

Day 13. What is King David's next question? Verse 4.

Time to Pay Your Debts

Ever make a promise to a good friend? Like, "If you let me have one of your brownies, I'll let you be pitcher next time we play ball." After you've eaten the brownie, you hope your friend forgets your promise because he's a terrible pitcher.

David had once made a promise to Jonathan. Now that Jonathan was dead he remembered the promise.

Day 14. Read 1 Samuel 20:12-17.

Day 15. What promise did Jonathan ask David to make in verse 15?

Day 16. How do we know David made that promise? Verse 17.

Day 17. What does David do when he discovers where Mephibosheth is now living? 2 Samuel 9:5.

Day 18. What is the reaction of Mephibosheth when he is brought to the court of King David? Verse 6.

Day 19. How do you think Mephibosheth felt in his heart when he faced King David? Verse 6 and start of verse 7.

Day 20. How does King David try to make Mephibosheth relax? Verse 7.

Day 21. What is King David going to do for Mephibosheth so that he can live like the grandson of a former king? Verse 7.

Day 22. How does Mephibosheth show that he is grateful for what King David has done? Verse 8.

Special Orders

Though Mephibosheth was the son of David's friend, he was the grandson of the man who had been Israel's first king. This meant he could have claimed to be Israel's real king at any time. Yet King David took him into his household and let him have his meals with the king's family. That's showing a lot of confidence. Then he also made it possible for Mephibosheth to live as a wealthy son of a royal family.

Day 23. Who did King David call in again? Who was Ziba? Verse 9.

Day 24. How do you think Ziba felt about his orders? I wonder if Ziba hadn't been running the farm as though it was his own!

Day 25. Who was to get all the profits from the farming operation now? Verse 10.

Day 26. How do we know that this was a large farm? Verse 10.

Day 27. What did Ziba say to King David in response to the orders he received? Verse 11.

Day 28. Did all the things King David promised really happen? Verse 13.

A Broken Promise

Day 29. What did Ziba do when King David was fleeing from his son Absalom? 2 Samuel 16:1-3.

Day 30. When King David asked why Mephibosheth was not in the group, what did Ziba say? Do you think Ziba was telling the truth? Verse 3.

Day 31. Read 2 Samuel 19:24-28. Now who had broken his promise? Why do you think Ziba deliberately told a lie about Mephibosheth? See 2 Samuel 16:4.

In this story we have seen how King David kept his word, but Ziba did not. In fact, Ziba betrayed Mephibosheth by lying about him so he could get the land and property. King David was a kind man and Ziba was a greedy man. God blessed King David, but Ziba had to give up what he had gained by deceit.

Is there someone you can be kind to today?

7

Outfoxing
the Hangman

David and Sue couldn't believe it.

"What a crabby old lady," Dave muttered, listlessly throwing the ball up in the air and catching it.

"Why didn't someone nice move in?" Sue asked, swinging at a tree branch with the bat.

The rest of the team caught up with them. "We ought to do something," exclaimed Steve, always ready for a good fight. "We'll make her sorry she doesn't let us play ball in her yard anymore."

The team members stood around waiting for someone to come up with a good idea.

"You'd think we had broken every window in her house," said Sandy. "Old man Smith sure was nice compared to her. Why did he have to sell the place anyway?"

He asked the question so sadly you knew he really didn't want an answer. Ever since they could remember, the kids in the neighborhood had played ball in the Smith's huge back yard. It was almost like a community playground, since the park was several blocks away. Now the new owner had chased them out of the yard and told them never to show up again.

The problem the team faced reminds me of the story in the Bible about Mordecai and Esther. Let's find out what that problem was and how they solved it.

Only Beautiful Girls Need Apply

Queen Vashti was the one who started all the trouble. When the king of Persia was nearing the end of a 180-day party, he decided to invite her to join them. After all, she was the most beautiful woman in all of Persia. He had personally selected her as his queen, and now was the time to show her off. But Queen Vashti refused to accompany the messengers back to the party. King Ahasuerus was so angry he immediately removed her as queen.

A few years later the king returned from a war in which he lost badly. He needed someone to cheer him up and remembered Vashti. It would have been too embarrassing to ask her to be queen again. One of his men had an idea.

Day 1.   What plan did the king's servant suggest? See Esther 2:2-4.

Day 2.   How did the king feel about the plan? Verse 4.

Day 3.   Who happened to be living in the capital city? Verse 5.

Day 4.   What had brought his great-grandfather to Susa, the capital of Persia? Verse 6.

Day 5.   What was Mordecai doing that showed he cared for those in his family? Verse 7.

Day 6.   What happened to Esther, his cousin? Verses 8 and 9.

Day 7.   What did Mordecai ask her to keep secret for the time being? Verse 10. How did he show he was very concerned about her? Verse 11.

Day 8.   Who was chosen to be the new queen of Persia? Verses 12-17.

Trouble At Court

"We simply can't let her get away with it," George spoke up firmly, looking back at the house. "Just wait until the Fourth of July. We can get all kinds of firecrackers and make her sorry she ever chased us away."

Steve brightened.

"That's a great idea. We'll get some rockets and scare her out of her wits," he said, starting to get excited.

Dave threw the ball a couple of feet higher, and reached out to catch it as it arched away from him.

"That doesn't get us back into her yard to play ball," he said. "She'll never let us back if we do that."

Let's get in on some scheming at the royal court in Persia!

Day 9.   Who was unhappy with the king of Persia? Verse 21.

Day 10.   Who discovered what they were planning to do? Verse 22. What was the plotters' unhappy ending? Verse 23.

Day 11.   Who became the most important man in Persia next to the king, and how did people have to show their respect? Chapter 3:1-2.

Day 12.   Somebody wasn't impressed. Who was he, and how did he show it? Verses 3-4.

Day 13.   What was Haman's reaction? How did he plan revenge against Mordecai and the other Jewish people in Persia? Verses 5-13.

Day 14.   How did Mordecai react to the new law? Chapter 4:1. How did the other Jewish people react? Verses 2-3.

Day 15.   What did Queen Esther do when she heard about the mourning among the Jews? Verses 4-5.

Day 16.   What did Mordecai ask Esther to do? Verses 6-8.

Day 17.   Did Esther think that she could help since she was queen? Verses 11-12.

Day 18.   How did Mordecai try to inspire Queen Esther to at least try to influence the king? Verses 13-14. On what condition did Queen Esther agree to do it? Verses 15-17.

Day 19.   How did the king react to Queen Esther's visit to the throne room? Chapter 5, verses 1-8.

Time For Revenge

"The Bible says we should not try to get even," Sue said, backing up Dave. "We need to think of some way to help her, not to get revenge."

Not everyone in the gang felt the way Sue and Dave did. They were in favor of scaring the new owner. Eventually the team members headed for home. That evening Dave told his father and mother about their bad experience with Mrs. Jamison.

"I wonder what would happen if you showed her kindness instead of trying to get even?" Mom wondered out loud.

Just as he was about to fall asleep that night, Dave had an idea.

Day 20.   What really upset Haman? Verses 9-13. What did his wife and friends suggest? Verse 14.

Day 21.   What happened when King Ahasuerus could not sleep at night? Chapter 6, verses 1-3.

Day 22.   Who was called in and what was he asked to do? Verses 4-10.

Day 23.   What did Haman do to Mordecai? Verses 11-12. Why was he so unhappy?

Day 24.   What discouraging things did Haman's wife say when she discovered that Mordecai was a Jew? Verse 13.

Day 25.   What did Queen Esther ask for when the king came to her banquet? Chapter 7, verses 2-4.

Day 26.   How did the king answer her? Verse 5. How did she identify the enemy of her people, the Jews? Verse 6.

Day 27.   How did Haman try to save his life? Verses 7 and 8. What did the king do when he saw Haman? Verse 8.

Day 28.   Haman had built gallows to hang Mordecai because he would not bow down to him. How were the gallows used? Verses 9-10.

Day 29.   How did the king now honor Mordecai and Queen Esther? Chapter 8, verses 1-4. What did Queen Esther ask for? Verses 5 and 6.

Day 30. What right did the king give to Mordecai? Verses 7 to 11.

Day 31. What is the happy ending? Verses 14-17.

The next day Dave went to Mrs. Jamison's house and knocked on the door. Mrs. Jamison kindly invited him in, got him a glass of milk, and started asking him about his parents and brothers and sisters.

Dave never told his teammates what went on in the house, but two weeks later they could be seen playing ball in the back yard again!

8

New Kid
on the Block

You're the big bright kid on the block. The other kids look up to you. When you tell them something, they listen. It's a great feeling.

Then a new family moves into a house on the block. And what should come out of the car but a kid bigger than you are. In two days you know you're in trouble. He has more exciting stories to tell, he can throw the ball further than you can, and he's got some new jokes that the other kids are listening to eagerly.

What now? Do you get a couple of kids together to wipe out the competition? Do you retreat to your TV room and forget about the kids? Or do you become one of the followers of the new kid?

That's kind of like the problem John the Baptist faced one day. Turn to John 1:19 and let's see what he did about it. But first open your Bible to chapter one of Mark.

Identification, Please

How popular are you? Depends on how many people want to listen to you, doesn't it? Or how many people want to see you come to bat in the baseball game . . . or pitch against the best team in the league.

Day 1. How popular was John the Baptist, the new preacher in the wilderness? Mark 1:4 and 5.

Day 3. How important did he think he was? Mark 1:7. Now turn to John chapter one.

Day 4. Who came to see what was going on in the wilderness, when the people should have been coming to the temple? John 1:19.

Day 5. Who did the priests and Levites think John might be? Verse 20.

Day 6. Who else did the Jewish leaders worry about? Verse 21.

Day 7. Now for the big question. What is it? Verse 22.

Day 8. Who did John say he was? Verse 23.

Day 9. What was John's job? Verse 23.

Setting the Trap

So how do you handle the kid who takes away your friends and robs you of your position? He's too big to fight, too smart to outwit. Set a trap in words so that he defeats himself?

Day 10. Who had sent the ones who were questioning Jesus? Do you get a little bit of the feeling that they didn't like the competition? Verse 24.

Day 11. Now that John the Baptist has said that he isn't one of the heroes come back to life, the

Pharisees ask for credentials. That's a big word for, "Who gave you the right to do what you are doing?" Read verse 25.

Day 12. How do we know that John the Baptist did not consider himself the most important man in town? Verses 26-27.

Day 13. Where did these things happen? Verse 28.

Who's Important Now?

Okay, so you are not the most important person on the block any more. It's hard to take, but facts are facts. Even if you imagine yourself leading the old gang, that doesn't make you the leader in real life. So you have to adjust. What did John the Baptist do?

Day 14. How does John describe Jesus? Verse 29.

Day 15. How does John know that Jesus is more important than he is? Verse 30.

Day 16. What sign did God give John the Baptist to help him recognize who Jesus really was? Verse 32.

Day 17. Who does John say Jesus is? Verse 34.

Day 18. How do we know that John was looked up to as an important teacher? Verse 35.

Day 19. What does John say about Jesus? Verse 36.

Day 20. What did the two disciples of John do? Verse 37.

A Better Leader

Can you imagine how John the Baptist must have felt? He had been the biggest attraction in the country, and suddenly all of his disciples left him to follow Jesus. No more security guards, no more security patrol, no more people to send on errands.

Day 21. What does Jesus ask the two men following him? Verse 38.

Day 22. What were they really looking for? Verse 38.

Day 23. What happens next? Verse 39.

Day 24. Give the name of one of the two young men who started following Jesus. Verse 40.

Day 25. What big news did Andrew bring his brother? Verse 41.

Day 26. What did Jesus have to say to the new convert? Verse 42.

Day 27. What happens when Jesus meets Philip? Verse 43.

Day 28. What was Philip's home city? Verse 44.

Day 29. What does Philip do? Verse 45.

Day 30. Who's the big sceptic? Verse 26.

Day 31. Where had Jesus seen Nathanael? Verse 48.

Day 32. What is Nathanael's response to the words of Jesus? Verse 49.

The disciples of John had followed him out into the wilderness because they knew he was an important person from the way he dressed and the way he could preach. But Jesus didn't have any special dress. He simply came along to be baptized by John in the river. Yet Jesus was the one who walked off with the disciples. And John learned that he had finished the biggest part of his life work. From now on the crowds would follow Jesus. And not once did John ever regain his prestige and power. So even if you get a bigger and brighter kid on your block, learn from him. Do the job God has given you . . . and do it well.

9

Bringing Along
a Brother

Eric picked up the ball as it rolled toward him, stepped back to the pitcher's mound he had made, and threw the baseball at the strike zone he had drawn on the garage. If only he could develop a special pitch. Then he might beat out his younger brother Sven.

It just isn't right, he thought to himself. *My brother is a whole year younger, yet he is taller.* Sven had made the grade seven baseball team, but Eric had failed to make the grade eight team. *Why did his younger brother always make it, and he didn't?*

He hitched up his pants, adjusted his baseball cap, and leaned forward as though waiting for a signal from the catcher. Then he straightened out, reared back, and threw the ball as hard as he could at the strike zone. *Strike two*, he said to himself, as the ball hit just inside the strike zone. *If I could*

75

only get three strikes on a real batter. Then Sven could hit as many home runs as he wanted and it wouldn't matter!

Good News for a Brother

Do brothers always have to compete with each other? Turn to John chapter one, beginning with verse 35.

Day 1.   How many of John's disciples were with him at this time? Verse 35.

Day 2.   What did they see happen? Verses 35 and 36.

Day 3.   What did the two disciples do? Verses 37-39.

Day 4.   What was the name of one of the disciples? Verse 40.

Day 5.   What was the good news that Andrew brought to his brother? Verse 41.

Day 6.   Where did Andrew take Simon, his brother? Verse 42.

Day 7.   What was Jesus' reaction when he saw Simon? Verse 42.

Day 8.   Who did Jesus recruit next? Verse 43.

Day 9.   How do we know that Philip knew Andrew and Simon Peter? Verse 44.

Day 10.   What did Philip do after Jesus asked him to follow Him? Verse 45.

Day 11.   Was Nathanael immediately ready to accept what his brother told him? Verse 46.

Day 12.   How did Philip prove to Nathanael that Jesus was "okay"? Verses 46 and 47.

Day 13.   What really convinced Nathanael that

Jesus was who his brother said he was? Verses 47-49.

A Good Testimony

"Hey, Eric, want to come along and play at the school?"

Sven had come around the corner of the house looking for his brother.

"Some of the guys are getting together for a game. I'm sure we could use a pitcher," he said.

I'll bet you can, so you can hit home runs off him, Eric thought to himself, but he picked up his ball and stuck his glove under his arm anyway. Anything was better than being alone.

What happens if your brother tries to help you? Let's follow Simon Peter through his life with Jesus.

Day 14. What was happening to Jesus? John 1:66.

Day 15. Was Jesus concerned? Verse 67.

Day 16. How does Peter answer Jesus' question? Verses 68 and 69. What does this tell us about Simon Peter, the brother of Andrew?

Several years have passed. Peter and Andrew are still following Jesus. Now Jesus has gathered them for their last meal together, although they do not know this will be their last supper with Jesus. Let's see what happens to Peter by exploring John 13.

Day 17. How do we know Jesus was aware that this was His last meal with the disciples? Verse 3 of chapter 13.

Day 18. What does Jesus do as an example of humble service? Verses 4 and 5.

Day 19. What does Simon Peter think about Jesus washing his feet? Verses 6-8.

Day 20. What does Peter want done if he has to have his feet washed by Jesus? Verse 9.

Day 21. Why does Jesus say that only Peter's dirty feet need washing? Verses 10 and 11.

Failing the Team

After the guys had warmed up by knocking out flies and playing some catch, sides were chosen for a team.

"Eric, I want you on my team," Sven said, picking his brother third. "I need a pitcher."

Being picked by his brother made Eric feel good. He hoped he would not fail him on the mound!

Let's look at a brother who failed the team. Turn to John 18:15.

Day 22.   What was the first mistake Peter made? Verse 15-17.

Day 23.   Where was Jesus taken after this? Verse 24.

Day 24.   What is Peter doing? Verse 25.

Day 25.   How many times did Peter deny that he was one of Jesus' followers? Verse 25-27.

Day 26.   What was the signal to Peter that reminded him of Jesus' warning? Verse 27.

Back on the Team

Sven's team was at bat first. They got off to a good start, with Sven hitting a home run with two men on base, and a total of five runs scoring.

"We got you a good lead, Eric," said Sven as he and Eric walked onto the field. "All we need is three men out. I'll catch anything coming my way . . . and I know you'll do great."

Eric roughed up the ball and started pitching. Though two runs scored, he did strike out one batter. And Sven caught a fly ball as promised, doubling a runner off second.

"Atta boy, Eric," he said, as he sat down beside his brother. "Next time we'll get 'em one-two-three."

What happened after Peter failed the team? Move to John 21:1.

Day 27.   Who was gathered together after the resurrection of Jesus? Verses 1 and 2.

Day 28.   Who made the suggestion to do what they had once done for a living? Verse 3.

Day 29.   What happened when Jesus came to visit? Verses 4-9.

Day 30.   What is the question Jesus asks Peter? Verses 15-17.

Day 31.   How do we know Peter is accepted by Jesus and is back on the team? Verses 15-17. Then read verses 18 and 19.

10

Making It Happen

Steve slammed one of his socks into the drawer angrily. Mom was in one of those "clean up your room before you can play" moods. He knew his friends would already be throwing the baseball around at the corner lot, and here he was picking up socks!

"If you don't learn to do a job well at home you will not do a good job away from home," his mother kept saying.

How well I clean up my room has nothing to do with how well I play ball, he thought angrily, as he picked up a pair of shorts and stuffed them into his drawer.

"You've got to learn to stick to what you are doing until you finish it," Mom said, as she walked by his bedroom, almost as if she had read his thoughts.

"Learn to be obedient," "Stick to what you have started," "Do your work well." "Don't let temptation keep you from what you know you should be doing."

Seems like Mom has a million things for me to learn and do, Steve thought as he hung up a pair of jeans.

"There, that looks better. Now you can play ball with the guys. You've done your work well," Mom said as she surveyed the room. She gave Steve a big hug.

A Concerned Officer

Steve knew what it meant to be stuck at home following his mother's orders, even though he wanted to go play ball. Let's check out someone who knew how to obey orders and keep at it until the work was done. *Read Luke 7:1-10.*

Day 1. What had Jesus been doing before he went to the city he now called home? Verse 1.

Day 2. What kind of a person was ill? Verse 2.

Day 3. How do we know the slave was appreciated? Verse 2.

Day 4. What was wrong with the slave at this time? Verse 2.

Day 5. A centurion was a Roman officer with 100 men under his command. The Jews did not like the Romans because they were the conquerors who controlled their country. Yet this centurion seems to have been someone special. What did the Jewish leaders do for him? Verse 3.

Day 6. What did the centurion want from Jesus? Verse 3.

Day 7. How do we know the Jewish leaders really liked the centurion? Verse 4.

Day 8. What had the centurion done that showed he was a kind man? Verse 5.

An Example of Obedience

Suppose Steve had said to himself, "Cleaning up my room is really a dumb thing. Even though Mom wants me to do it, I'm not going to do it. I'll just sit on my bed for as long as it would take me to do it, and then I'll sneak out." Do you think he would have gotten away with it? Would he have learned the lesson his mother was trying to teach him? Our story about the centurion helps us understand a little more about that.

Day 9. How do we know Jesus was willing to help the centurion? Verse 6.

Day 10. Where was Jesus when the centurion sent another message to him? Verse 6.

Day 11. What didn't the centurion want Jesus to do? Verse 6.

Day 12. Why didn't the centurion go to meet Jesus himself? Verse 7.

Day 13. What did the centurion want Jesus to do? Verse 7.

Day 14. How do we know the centurion was used to having his orders obeyed? Verse 8.

Day 15. How had the slave who was ill carried out his duties? Verse 8.

Day 16. What was Jesus' response to the message from the centurion's friends? Verse 9.

Day 17. What did Jesus say, indicating the centurion's faith was special? Verse 9.

Day 18. What happened to the slave who was ill? Why? Verse 10.

The Results of Obedience

When Steve got to the corner lot, Jack (his friend Bill's big brother) was teaching the guys how to pick up a grounder. He was barking out orders as if he was a drill sargeant in the army. Soon Steve was caught up in it, hustling to his left then to his right. Without realizing it, he was taking orders without even stopping to think whether they were good or not. If only his mother could have seen it!

Peter and his friends got into a situation where Jesus gave them an order. How they responded determined the reward. *Read about it in Luke 5:1-11.*

Day 19. What was Jesus doing beside the lake? Verse 1.

Day 20. What else was happening along the shore of the lake? Verse 2.

Day 21. Whose boat did Jesus get into? Verse 3.

Day 22. What did Jesus ask Simon Peter to do so He could speak to more people at once? Verse 3. Have you ever noticed how far you can hear voices when they are on the water?

Day 23. What did Jesus tell Simon Peter to do when He finished talking to the people? Verse 4.

Day 24. What had happened during the night before? Verse 5.

Day 25. Why was Simon Peter willing to try to catch some fish even though they had not been able to catch any the night before? Verse 5.

Day 26. How many fish did they catch when they obeyed Jesus' order? Verse 6.

Day 27. Whom did they ask to help them bring the fish to shore? Verse 7.

Day 28. How do we know they caught many more fish than usual? Verse 7.

Day 29. What did Simon Peter do that shows he realized Jesus had done something special? Verse 8.

Day 30. What kind of new job did Jesus promise the fishermen? Verse 10.

Day 31. How do we know the disciples believed Jesus? Verse 11.

By the time Steve had stopped about fifty grounders and thrown them to first base, he was pretty good at it. Doing it over and over gave him not only the right movements but the self-confidence to do it right. He had made up his mind he would stick to it until he could play his position well.

And who knows? Maybe Steve's determination to do something well would spill over into every-day chores too!

11

The Mouth Strikes Again

"My fort is stronger than anyone else's."

Jason turned and looked around with that knowing air he sometimes put on. Lunch was over and the students were waiting for the bell to ring so they could go back to the classroom. As usual, Jason was bragging about what he had done.

"My father's an engineer, and he helped me build it."

The bell finally rang and Jim quickly headed for the classroom. He could take only so much of the fat kid's bragging. It seemed like every time the guy opened his mouth he was telling how great he or something he made was. Maybe some of the things he made were better, but did he have to brag about them all the time?

Going for a Walk

Seems every class has at least one "mouth," someone who's always bragging and showing off. Believe it or not, the Bible tells about a man whose mouth continually led the way. A man named Peter had a habit of engaging his mouth before he put his brain in gear. In fact, he probably embarrassed the other disciples terribly. Let's see how Jesus treated "The Mouth." Turn to Matthew 14:22-32.

Day 1.   What did Jesus ask the disciples to do? Verse 22.

Day 2.   Where did Jesus go when His disciples left the boat? Verse 23.

Day 3.   What happened when the disciples were alone on the boat? Verse 24.

Day 4.   What did Jesus do in the middle of the storm? Verses 25 and 26.

Day 5.   How did the disciples feel when they saw the figure on the water? Verse 26.

Day 6.   How did Peter respond when he heard Jesus' reassuring words? Verse 27. How do you think the other disciples felt when they heard Peter? Can't you hear one of them saying. "There he goes again, making a fool of himself?"

Day 7.   What happened to Peter when he walked toward Jesus? Verses 29-30. How do you think the disciples felt when they saw "The Mouth" sinking?

Day 8.   How did Jesus react? Verse 31. Did Jesus blame Peter for doing a foolish thing?

Right On, Peter

After school Jim rode his bike to Jason's house.

He had to see for himself if Jason's fort was so great. When he arrived, Jason was working at one of the spots, adding more snow.

"Hi, Jim, want to help?"

That wasn't really why Jim had come. In fact, he had absolutely no desire to help Jason. But he figured maybe he could learn something from him. And guess what? Jason didn't mind showing Jim the things his engineer father had taught him. As a result Jim realized that there was usually some truth to Jason's big talk.

Let's check in on Peter again in Matthew 16:13-17.

Day 9. What was Jesus trying to find out from His disciples? Verse 13.

Day 10. What are some of the answers? Verse 14.

Day 11. What answer does Peter give? Verse 16.

Day 12. How does Jesus react to Peter's words? Verse 17.

Day 13. Yet like most braggarts, Peter could not leave it alone when he said something that was really true. Read on in chapter 16, from verse 21.

Day 14. What did Jesus say would happen to Him when He went to Jerusalem? Verse 21.

Day 15. What did Peter say to Jesus when he heard this? Verse 22. Why do you think Peter was so upset?

Day 16. How do we know Peter had really put his foot in his mouth this time? Verse 23.

Day 17. In other words, Peter was more interested in his own glory than in seeing Jesus die for man's sin. What word do we use to describe such an attitude? It begins with s.

Day 18.   What attitude are we to have as Christians? Verse 24.

Trapped Again

As they were working on the fort, Jason suddenly said, "I bet a bulldozer couldn't push this fort over. It's so strong."

Jim knew better than to laugh, for Jason was bigger and stronger. But he also knew that no snow fort could stand up against a bulldozer. Suddenly he remembered something.

"I'll bet it won't stay when the sun shines warm on it in spring," he said.

Jason knew he had been trapped.

"You're right," he said. Suddenly his fort didn't seem so strong anymore.

Peter thought he was very strong too. Let's see how strong he really was when Jesus was taken prisoner. Turn to Matthew 26:31.

Day 19.   What did Jesus say would happen? Verse 31.

Day 20.   How did Peter react when he heard this? Verse 33.

Day 21.   What would be the signal showing that Peter would have to "eat his words?" Verse 34.

Day 22.   How sure was Peter that this would not happen to him? Verse 35.

Day 23.   Where was Peter when Jesus was on trial in the house of the high priest? Verse 69.

Day 24.   Who pointed Peter out as being a disciple of Jesus? Verse 69.

Day 25.   Did "The Mouth" tell the truth this time?

Verse 70. What does Peter's answer show us about his courage?

Day 26. Who spoke to Peter next? What did she say? Verse 71. What was Peter's reaction?

Day 27. How did another bystander identify Peter as a disciple of Jesus? Verse 73. How did Peter react this time? Verse 74.

Day 28. How do we know Peter realized he had been trapped by his bragging? Verse 75.

Down But Not Out

Jim could see Jason's disappointment. Suddenly he realized that Jason talked a lot, but wasn't unbeatable. He surprised himself by saying, "That's okay. Next winter I'll help you build another fort.

And we can ask some of the other guys to help us."

Jesus also took time out to show Peter love even though he was often an embarrassment to have around. Read about it in John 21:15-19.

Day 29.   What question did Jesus ask Peter three times? Verses 15, 16, 17.

Day 30.   How do we know Jesus accepted Peter's expression of his love? Verses 15, 16, 17. He gave Peter a big job to do after Jesus was gone, didn't he? You see, one way to let another person know you love him is to ask him to do something special for you.

Is there a "mouth" in your class or group? Does anyone you know do something that drives you crazy or makes you feel uncomfortable? If you really love Jesus, you'll follow His example and love "unlovable" people too!

12

More Than a Garage Sale

The sky was dark and the clouds hung low as I walked into our garage, a couple of "Garage Sale" posters under one arm and some nails and hammer in the other. I selected a couple of long stakes, sharpened them and attached the signs.

Today the young people of the church were having a garage sale to raise money for a missionary project. As the father of a couple of teens, I had been asked to put up the signs my son had prepared (he was working on a summer job). I had just put up the signs when the rain came. Soon the soft paper posterboard drooped badly – but the sale went on.

Next Sunday the pastor announced that the garage sale had raised $250 for the missionary project. That's when it hit me. The garage sale had been successful, but none of the teens had given anything. All they had done was share what their parents couldn't use anymore and were ready to throw away. But the Bible talks about us sharing of ourselves and what we own. That's more than having a garage sale!

The man who wrote the book of Luke in the Bible was a doctor. More than any other writer he tells about the sick people Jesus healed. But he also gives us more examples than anyone else of people who needed to share. That's because he saw the needs of the poor people so clearly.

Let's go on a voyage of discovery in Luke and see how we can share with others as we begin to see poor people through the eyes of Jesus.

Wrong Kind of Crop

We were driving past field after field of soybeans. Some of them looked absolutely beautiful. But every so often we would see one where there seemed to be more weeds than soybeans. That's the wrong kind of crop! Jesus told the story of a man who also planted lots of seeds.

Day 1. Read Luke 12:13-14. This is the introduction to the story Jesus will tell. What is the important thing Jesus wants to teach us? See verse 14 especially.

Day 2. Now read Luke 12:15-21. How had God blessed the man whose story Jesus told?

Day 3. What big problem faced this happy farmer? See verse 17.

Day 4. What does he decide to do? Verse 18.

Day 5. Since he was now rich, this farmer felt he could enjoy life without worrying about anything.

So how will he spend the rest of his life? Verse 19.
Day 6. What had the rich man overlooked?
Verse 20.
Day 7. What lesson is Jesus trying to teach with
this story? Verse 21. Compare this with verses
22-23.
Day 8. This man had grown a crop of greed,
wanting more and more. God was looking for a
crop of thankfulness. What kind of crop do you
have? See verse 33 for the kind of treasure Jesus
asks us to collect.

No Sale for Him

Day 9. Read Luke 18:18-24. The same story is
reported in Matthew 19:16-24. How old was the
religious leader?
Day 10. What is the most important question
ever asked Jesus? Verse 18 of Luke 18.
Day 11. How good are we when we compare
ourselves with God? Verse 19.
Day 12. How good did the rich young ruler think
he was? Verse 20.
Day 13. Do you think the man could really say
he had kept every commandment? Don't you think
he might have done just a little bit wrong? See
James 2:10.
Day 14. What does Jesus ask the rich young man
to do? Verse 22.
Day 15. If you were rich and Jesus asked you
to sell everything and give it to the poor, what
would you do? What did the rich young ruler do?
Verse 23.

Day 16.   What does Jesus say about rich people? Verse 24. Do you think it is just as difficult today for rich men to believe in Jesus and follow Him? Why? Could it be because rich people have so much they do not think they need Jesus?

Day 17.   The rich young ruler decided he did not want to have a big sale. He felt he had every right to enjoy all the good things he had earned. Do we have a right to be rich when one-third of the people in the world do not have enough to eat today? The next story Jesus told shows us a man who probably was rich, but he didn't keep it all to himself.

Sharing More than Money

Day 18.   Read Luke 10:30-37. The Jews and Samaritans disliked each other. In fact, the Jews would not even travel through Samaria if they could help it.

Day 19.   What happened to the Jewish traveler? Do people today ever get into that kind of trouble?

Day 20.   Who was the first traveler to notice the beaten-up man? See verse 31. What kind of reaction did he have?

Day 21.   The badly-beaten man was probably still moaning and groaning when another man came along. What did he do? See verse 32. At least he stopped to take a good look. Maybe he suddenly realized that the bandits might still be in the area.

Day 22.   What is the first reaction of the Samaritan? Verse 33.

Day 23.   The Samaritan did more than feel sorry for the wounded man. He took time to do what? Verse 34.

Day 24. Read verse 34 again. What are the important things the Samaritan shared with the wounded man? Would you say he shared time, medicine, and energy? What can you share with someone in need?

Day 25. Yet the Samaritan shared more than most of us would have expected. Read verse 35 and list what else he shared.

Day 26. What is the lesson Jesus wants to teach us? See verses 36 and 37. Who is your neighbor? What can you share? Maybe you do not have a lot of money to give, but when you share your time with a friend who is ill, when you help out a neighbor lady with her garbage when she has the flu, when you help Dad out with something on the farm or around the house when he is not feeling well, then you are being neighborly.

You Don't Have to be Rich

Day 27.   The Apostle Paul had visited the church in Corinth. They had promised to give some money to help poor people in Jerusalem. In his letter to them he reminds them of their promise. What churches does he mention as a good example? Read 2 Corinthians 8:1-2.

Day 28.   Most of us give the pennies or dimes left over after buying candy and stuff. How much did the people in the churches in Macedonia give? See verse 3.

Day 29.   Why did they want the Apostle Paul to take the money? Verse 4.

Day 30.   What was the most important thing these people did before they shared their money? Verse 5.

Day 31.   Think about this. God is more interested in you as a person than in your money. He wants you to give yourself to Him because He loves you. But when you give yourself to Jesus He will also share in everything you have. What does Jesus say about helping others in Matthew 10:40-42?